Becoming Wife
Hindsight!

The Choice to See it.

By Valerie J. Pacheco

June 23, 2025

Copyright 2025 by Valerie J. © Pacheco – All rights reserved.

It is not legal to reproduce, duplicate, or transmit any part of this document in either electronic or printed format. Recording this publication is strictly prohibited.

Library of Congress Control Number: 2025913411

Contents

Emails & Socials 4
Introduction 5
Closet, Cross, & Me 8
True Forgiveness 44
Modeling & Morals 64
Trauma Meets Love 88
Becoming 111
My Lane 122
Conclusion 137
About the Author (With Links) 154
Written, edited, & manufactured by Valerie J. Pacheco 156

Emails & Socials

 @GS.ValerieP

 @i.am.my.ancestors6

 @valeriefbAuthor

 @GSNaturals

 goodstuff.natural@gmail.com

 seedsnwla@gmail.com

Introduction

Becoming Wife: Hindsight! The Choice to See It. is an honest and deeply personal reflection on the journey of growing into the role of a wife—not just by title, but in heart, spirit, and character. Rooted in the biblical truth that "he who finds a wife finds a good thing," this book explores what it really means to be that good thing, especially when you don't start out feeling like one.

With transparency, faith, and a touch of humor, the author shares how becoming a wife is less about the wedding day and more about the refining process—learning selflessness, emotional maturity, and the value of meaningful relationships. Through hard-earned lessons, moments of conviction, and divine revelation, she invites women to see their own process with grace and to choose growth over guilt, wisdom over wounds, and purpose over perfection.

Becoming is a choice—and hindsight can be your greatest teacher.

QR code for website and socials. Please leave a review.

Closet, Cross, & Me

In 2005, I was working at the Southern Maid Donut shop on Hearne Avenue. The aftermath of Hurricane Katrina brought hundreds of survivors to Independence Stadium, and our shop was serving many of them. Because of this, my boss scheduled several of us for double shifts. While the extra hours meant a bigger paycheck, the toll on my body was significant, my feet and back ached with exhaustion.

It was just a few minutes past midnight when I finally made it home. I unlocked the deadbolt and carefully turned the doorknob to enter the cute little blue house that I shared with my boyfriend. As I walked toward the bedroom, ready to put my things down and unwind, an unusual sound caught my attention. It sounded like someone was quietly shuffling a small laundry basket of clothes across the bedroom floor.

I saw that my dog was coming from the bedroom, the problem was that she wasn't barking. The thing is, Madam wasn't one of those dogs that was friendly with everyone. She was an aggressive girl. Madam's coat was all white, she was a gorgeous Red Nose American pit bull.

I looked at Madam, and she looked at me as if to tell me, hi mom, someone we know is in the room. So, I quietly pulled out my phone and called 911. I explained to the operator that I had just come home from a double shift, and I heard a sound, but my dog is not barking.

The 911 operator instructed me unlock the front door and to take my dog and myself into the bathroom, and to lock the door. It was about 5 minutes that passed when I heard the police knock on the door, I heard "Shreveport police", then they entered into the front door with a canine, moments later I heard the police canine barking.

Surprisingly, Madam was well behaved, I think she knew and was just trying to keep me safe. I was able to hear the police officers and the canine in the bedroom, suddenly, I heard that boyfriend of mine yell, "this is my house, this is my house", he was asleep in the closet, whoa, that's nuts! Why would he be asleep in the closet?! The police officers questioned him; he explained that he just fell asleep in the closet.

It was wild to me, why on earth would he be hiding in the closet?! One of the police officers pulled me aside to speak to me about my safety, he said to me that he did not believe that that man just decided to nap in the closet. The officer also stated that he had a daughter about my age, and he was worried that my boyfriend was trying to kill me because my boyfriend also had a gun with him in that closet.

Of course, being young I did not listen to the officer, and the excuse is that I did not believe that that man would kill me, I couldn't think of a reason why. Yet it bugged me that he was asleep in the closet with a gun. "What happened that night shook me. But instead of clarity, it left me with more questions than answers."

As time went on, I asked my grandmother what I should do about the relationship that I was in because something didn't feel right.

My grandmother told me to pray to God to reveal that man's true face. Not much time passed between that prayer and when I saw the demon in his face laughing at me.

    That moment in time marks the beginning of me trying to understand who I am and what is my purpose, why am I here, am I meant to be abused, misused, misguided, like what is the purpose?! Have you ever wondered about these things?

As I began to read my Bible trying to learn from the perspective of godly word, I was searching for my identity, I was searching for the purpose that I have here in the world and trying to understand what am I supposed to be doing, how do I stay out of danger, and how do I become a person that is lovable?

I couldn't help but ask Yeshua why me? Why Yah, what have I done that I have to continue to suffer, why must my heart ache, no one loves me, I have no idea where my children are, and I have to look in the mirror at something that I don't understand.

I continued to pursue an understanding of self and to grow through the pain that I was feeling. Although it was fake when I would smile, those fake smiles got me through. My job and my siblings were my comfort zone, and it stayed that way for many years.

With my job I was able to pretend to have a better life and to feel better about myself, that was similar to school for me. I can go there, and I can just mask all the pain with jokes and laughter, and it makes life easier to bear. And with my siblings it became a numbing agent for my scars because they understood me to a certain extent, they knew what I had been through, But I did not know what they were going through.

So, when the conversations came up with me and my siblings about the things that took place, the things that had scarred me actually traumatized them as well. They helped me to realize that I was not the only one suffering and that I was not the only one with uncomfortable memories. This taught me empathy.

It seems to me that when you are victimized, especially in childhood, that the things done against that person, or child, will cause that victim to lose bits and pieces of self, and it harms those that are close to that person. I believe that this is because our bodies and brains have to figure out a way to ease the hurt. We develop different ways of coping; my way became Jack Daniels whiskey in my Coca-Cola. I carried those spiked Coca-Cola bottles everywhere I went, even at school, and I started that bad habit at only 12 years old. Thankfully I was never caught.

Another way I learned to cope with being sexually abused was lying. I lied about small things about myself, you know, things like, "are you happy", or "how was your day", or "what's been going on". My answers would always be "I'm fine", or "I'm good", and "blessed and highly favored".

    Another problem that I was facing was when it came to my looks. I had watched The Color Purple, and I remember that Ceely Was called ugly, yet her stepfather had previously molested her, getting her pregnant twice then giving her babies away. "Then her stepfather handed her over to Mister, a widower who was obsessed with Shug Avery." Both men used her for sex. Mister really wanted her little sister, Nettie and was forced to take Ceely, so her being his wife was merely her being his servant and concubine, taking care of his house and his children. So, I equated that to mean that I was ugly.

She wasn't ugly to me, nor was I, but because our skin colors were the same, we both hid our smiles, and we both had some vile older man humping on us. I figured; I'm just like Ceely.

This feeling of ugliness started with the movie, but as I grew, I saw and felt how being a dark skin girl was not going to be easy. The whole lighter brighter better thing was big in the 1990s, and in all honesty, it is still kind of prevalent today. And maybe it's still a thing today because dark skin people still feel a bit uncomfortable in our skin due to ignorant comments and judgments some people make.

June 2005, when I met the man that fathered my two youngest children, the guy who swooped in to hold me as I healed. We got married on Valentine's Day 2007, as I write this, we've now celebrated our 18th anniversary this year, 2025.

This Proverbs 31 woman in the Bible had become a guiding light for me.

Proverbs 31:10-31 NKJV;

Who can find a virtuous wife?
For her worth is far above rubies.
The heart of her husband safely trusts her;

So he will have no lack of gain.
She does him good and not evil
All the days of her life.
She seeks wool and flax,
And willingly works with her hands.
She is like the merchant ships,
She brings her food from afar.
She also rises while it is yet night,
And provides food for her household,
And a portion for her maidservants.
She considers a field and buys it;
From her profits she plants a

vineyard.

She girds herself with strength,
And strengthens her arms.
She perceives that her merchandise is good,
And her lamp does not go out by night.
She stretches out her hands to the distaff,
And her hand holds the spindle.
She extends her hand to the poor,
Yes, she reaches out her hands to the needy.

She is not afraid of snow for her household,
For all her household is clothed with scarlet.
She makes tapestry for herself;
Her clothing is fine linen and purple.
Her husband is known in the gates,
When he sits among the elders of the land.
She makes linen garments and
She opens her mouth with wisdom,
And on her tongue is the law of

kindness.

She watches over the ways of her household,

And does not eat the bread of idleness.

Her children rise up and call her blessed;

Her husband also, and he praises her:

"Many daughters have done well,

But you excel them all."

Charm is deceitful and

beauty is passing,

But a woman who fears the Lord, she shall be praised.
Give her of the fruit of her hands, And let her own works praise her in the gates.

I read that and said, "Yes, I can model myself after this description".

The problem with that ideal was that I'm not some perfect virtuous woman, I am flawed, I mess up sometimes, and I am normal. It is true that I possess a few of those qualities, but I had to discover me, which would take time, a lot of time.

Over the course of twenty years, one thing I've realized is that sometimes you have to take a step back to learn, grow up, and gain perspective. Rushing to be in control of everything spells disaster in the long run. Becoming wife is a process of respect, commitment, and selflessness.

Sadly, I had nobody in my life that enlightened me about the complexities of marriage, or I failed to take heed and therefore don't remember, either or, I was sure to find out the hard way.

One of my shortcomings in the beginning of mine and my husband's union was my being outwardly selfless, but selfish and guarded in the ways that matter for marriage. See, I was great at keeping up appearances, I took good care of our babies, the house was clean, clothes washed, food cooked, and things were nice.

But I was loud with my opinions and easy to offend, even though I claimed to like how blunt my husband was. From the moment I met him, he was always very frank, and he never pretended to be anything other than himself.

I was the one pretending to be something I wasn't, I didn't know it, but time sure enough showed me that I did not know myself and that having an identity would be more challenging than trying to hold everything together.

FYI, being married to someone that says what they mean and mean what they say is pretty tough for a person who is lost. Nearly everything he said began to offend me and as a young immature girl, the only way I knew how to feel better was to call out his flaws and vent to my family members about it.

    Focusing on my feelings and desires was all I knew, and this is why I had to take some time out to pray, listen, and obey the biblical principles I was learning, but I didn't do that right away. In all honesty, it took me several years to learn some of the most important lessons about becoming a wife.

Before I tell you all about it, how about I first explain what I mean when I say, "Becoming Wife", and what I have come to believe a "Wife" is exactly. I have been married, on paper, ever since February 14th, 2007, but I don't know exactly how long I've been a wife in the eyes of Yeshua. The wife part sometimes escaped me. Don't get me wrong, I knew all the stuff the good television shows taught us about marriage, like have some babies and be a great mom, cook, clean, smile, and make nice.

    Having the being, the heart, and the mindset of wife was the missing formula that kept me in constant conflict and agony throughout many years of marriage. See, I had the knowledge of wifely duties and the basic understanding of how it looked to be a wife, but I lacked any amount of wisdom to truly be the wife I thought I was being.

Becoming Wife is growing from girl to woman, we learn, we embody, we change, we blossom into the flower that is Wife. We do this by keeping the knowledge we learn and finding the biblical balance, and that gives us some Godly wisdom.

I realize that some people do not like, and may even despise the fact that religious people, or like me, believers of the Word, are always referring to the bible, well friend, I would say that the bible is the whole reason we get married, I mean hello, our heavenly Father created marriage, and most of us repeated the biblical vows during our ceremonies, therefore the word of Yahweh is far more relevant than people's feelings.

And that, was my biggest problem in my own marriage, I got sick and tired of folks telling me about what the bible says about marriage. I felt like, if he isn't a biblical husband, why does he deserve a biblical wife.

I kept praying for my husband to be fixed, and for him to change. I didn't understand why my prayers seemed to go unanswered.

Have you ever watched the movie Not Easily Broken? During the couple's wedding, the officiator said that marriage is a three-strand cord, the husband, the wife, and God. That was absolutely beautiful to me, but I didn't know how to make my marriage be like that, and obviously, they didn't either.

True Forgiveness

"When Anger Won't Leave"

Have you ever experienced such profound anger that it seemed impossible to forgive those who caused you harm, suffering, and emotional or mental distress? I have, and it is truly challenging. The issue I faced was that, according to the teachings of the Bible and other literature, true peace could not be achieved without forgiveness. This forgiveness required an internal struggle and learning to trust Yahweh, as I could not forgive as easily as I had anticipated.

I realized that my anger was directed towards many individuals: my mother, my father, the person who victimized me, everyone who knew but did not assist, myself, and even Yahweh. What was I to do with all this anger? Time taught me valuable lessons, especially when life presents hardships and one prays for guidance. One must be prepared to face what they have prayed for. "Honestly, I wasn't ready for the test that came with the prayer."

"When I Prayed for Change…"

"Father, please help me not to be angry, help me to be more patient, help me to be a better mother, and fix my husband as he is mean and curses excessively. In Jesus' name, Amen."

"To me, the prayer seemed simple and reasonable. But I've learned that Yahweh often answers our prayers in ways that stretch us — not comfort us."

When I prayed to help me manage my anger, He provided situations that tested my patience and tolerance. When I sought assistance in becoming more patient, circumstances arose to teach me patience. When I prayed to become a better mother, I received numerous opportunities to improve in that role.

Regarding my husband, I learned that it was not my place to ask Yahweh to change him; it was up to my husband to seek change through his own relationship with our heavenly Father. Nevertheless, I could pray for his overall well-being, healing, protection, and prosperity, but his personal relationship with Yah was his own responsibility.

During this period, I continued to experience anger and resentment. I was unaware that the aspects of oneself that need change through prayer are challenges that will persist until one learns to release them to our Savior, trusting that He will help.

As time went on, my frustration grew because I felt I was not making progress. I believed I was doing everything correctly, only to realize that I was mistaken. At times, I assumed a stance of righteousness and indulged in self-pity, which eventually alienated others. I began to have solitary pity parties, which exacerbated my feelings of loneliness.

It was then that I started conversing with Yeshua sincerely, asking Him how to overcome these emotions and what was wrong with me. I always ended my prayers with two requests: "Father, please hold my hand and guide me in my blindness, I do not know what I am doing, but I trust You," and "Please cover and protect my children."

    Regarding the anger towards my parents, I heard someone suggest that parents who evoke negative feelings in their children might also harbor similar feelings towards their own parents, and that they too may have been victims in their lives.

    This insight prompted me to reflect on some of the hurtful things my parents had said to me about their life experiences, and what they had each shared about being in relationship with one another. Although their past pain does not excuse their behavior, it allowed me to extend grace and empathy, making forgiveness easier.

Forgiving myself was unusual, requiring me to learn self-love, starting with daily affirmations in the mirror. Looking into my bathroom mirror, I repeatedly told myself, "I love you; you are worthy of love, you are loved." This practice had a powerful effect on me, initially bringing tears, but over time, I was able to do it without crying.

"Forgiving the Unforgivable"

Forgiving the person who harmed me demanded considerable effort and work. This part may be the most difficult in my path to real forgiveness. First, don't get me wrong, forgiving is by no means forgetting. That was one of the major issues I faced when I had been told 'forgive and forget'. That phrase used to make me plain mad because I never could understand how folks expected for me to forget, I cannot forget.

"An elder once told me, 'Forgive, but never forget — because forgetting opens the door to repeated harm.' That advice made far more sense to me than 'forgive and forget.' So, I forgave— or at least I thought I did."

Here's how I found out I had not forgiven that man at all. About two years ago, I was at home cleaning, when I heard the Holy Spirit say, "tell him you forgive him". Immediately, I said, "nah, I ain't doing that".

Oh, did you know that the Holy Spirit will raise his voice in a very stern manner?

Well, for me this was the second time in less than a year that I heard that small and calm voice raised up in me. I heard the same thing a second time, "tell him you forgive him".

A couple of weeks later, I finally called my baby brother Joshua to ask for that man's phone number. I told my brother the whole spill, he said wow, then he gave me the number. It took me a couple of days to get nerve up to send a text message asking for permission to call and talk.

When I did, there was no response. I asked Josh if he was sure that he gave me the right number, he assured me that he did. So, I waited a few more days to send another text message, nothing.

Not knowing what to do, I called Uncle Greg, that's my dad's younger brother, and one thing about my uncle, he's gonna give it to me straight, no chaser. My uncle is also sound in biblical doctrine, so when I get stuck on these type of things he is an amazing and wise elder to have.

After explaining everything to Uncle Greg and telling him how even though I never got to tell that man that I forgive him, I felt free of the whole thing, and that I just did not understand. Uncle Greg said, "maybe, God was testing you to see If you would be obedient".

"The Abraham Test"

Immediately, I thought about Yahweh testing Abraham when he told him to sacrifice his son Issac.

Abraham didn't want to do that, Issac was his heir, his only legitimate son. I cannot imagine how he initially felt when Yahweh told him to do that.

Abraham's ultimate test of faith appears in Genesis 22:1-18, where Yahweh directs him to sacrifice his son Isaac. Despite the unimaginable request, Abraham responded with immediate obedience, showing his unwavering faith.

At the critical moment on Mount Moriah, an angel intervened, telling him to spare his son, and there was a ram stuck in the thicket to take Isaac's place.

This powerful moment demonstrates how surrendering fully to biblical teaching—even when it's difficult—opens the way for divine provision and reveals the depth of true faith.

"The Peace That Came"

Thinking of it in that way caused me to believe, while hoping I *sells them,*
And supplies sashes for the merchants.
Strength and honor are her clothing;
She shall rejoice in time to come.

am correct in this belief, that because I felt free of it once I tried to do what the Holy Spirit told me to do, that Uncle Greg is right, I was being tested, and because I was obedient, even though I stumbled, that the burden of unforgiveness was removed from me. I think it is so because even now, I do not feel anger toward that man, I remember fully, the remembrance doesn't feel agonizing anymore, and it no longer causes me to cry or feel anxious. For that, I am most grateful.

"And now I know — forgiveness doesn't always start with feeling; sometimes it starts with obeying, obedience of the word of our Creator."

Modeling & Morals

Not long before my 20th birthday, I was living in Carrolton, Texas with my big brother, Marcus and his wife, my sis, Stephanie.

During that time, I decided to take the advice of some of my family members, so I went to pursue modeling. One reason I chose to go for it is because I had fun back in the day, high school, in 9th grade at Manual Arts High School in Los Angeles, California, I joined a modeling club after school.

I was told that I was too short for the runway so I didn't believe that modeling was for me, but since my family and some acquaintances were so persistent in telling me I should, I went for it.

I can't recall the name of the modeling agency that I chose to begin building my portfolio, but I recall Stephanie and I going there together.

As the photographer wrapped up and I was about to get dressed there were two White men approaching, dressed in very nice-looking suits, and carrying briefcases. It felt as if they were about to approach me, and I felt vulnerable, but I knew that whatever they were about to ask of me, my response would be no. "I couldn't explain it, but that was one of the clearest 'no's' I've ever known."

The men showed me and Stephanie some of the most teensy-weensy bikinis, as small as

I was, I didn't see me fitting my lady bits into the various strings and those bits being covered. They offered to pay something like $3000 per photo, that sounded strange. Sis said, "if I had your little figure, I'd take that offer".

The money didn't matter, and I was broke, but I knew what the answer was, no, that's not for me! It was clear in my mind, and I told the guys that I hope to be someone's grandmother one day, I don't want them seeing or being embarrassed by old pictures of their granny.

When My Body Broke Down

Fast forward, between 2011 and 2014, married with a baby and a toddler, I felt the strongest desire to change my life after battling a very difficult battle with three bleeding ulcers in my stomach and intestine.

For years I had been quite literally surviving on 4 to 8 Ibuprofen and several Coca-Cola's each day, and sometimes garbage foods like Down Home smoked sausages, cheese puffs, gas station pizza, and other times two or three of my kids Dino Nuggets. I didn't eat much at all, even at family functions.

I also smoked about 1 ½ packs of Cools cigarettes per day.

Corona was my beer of choice, and Remy Martin or 1800 Tiquila was the main liquor I liked to drink. Yeah, I enjoyed partying and hitting a good club or bar. My weight stayed around 100 pounds, and I thought my size was normal because my mom is a small woman.

On one very frightful night, I woke up to go tinkle. When I wiped, I looked at to toilet paper and thought dang, it's very heavy. As I looked in the toilet, it looked like an abnormal amount of blood, but I didn't think that it was anything life threatening.

So, I grabbed a pad, cleaned up and got myself together. When I stood up to go back to bed, "BAM!" I hit the floor. My husband awoke and sat up in bed, asking, "what happened, are you okay?" I said, yeah, I'm fine, as I picked myself up to continue on to bed, then, "BAM!" I hit the floor again. From there he jumped up, got out of bed to help me, and said, "hell no, you're going to the hospital."

He got our toddlers up and by the front door, it was so scary for him, Myah and Ricardo were probably too young to really be afraid, but our little son, who hadn't even turned 3-years-old yet, took my right hand and walked slowly with me as my husband holding me upright guided us all to the car.

I will gladly spare you the details of the hospital staff learning that the prognosis was bleeding ulcers, but I will tell you that I was so ashamed, I cried and cried. My nurse was so kind; I kept apologizing to her as I bawled my eyes out.

Something you should know about me is that I was always

afraid of not doing things just right, which I believe to be a result of fearing my stepfather, and that level of stress added to him molesting me for years paired with my unhealthy junk food and beverage choices, oh, and those ibuprofen, was probably what triggered the development of the ulcers.

    I was so afraid that I couldn't have disagreement with my

husband without picturing getting back handed in my mouth. Sadly, that was not the only thing I projected onto my spouse.

Soon after recovering we moved to a little house not far from my mom and Tyrone.

"By the way, Tyrone— who is my mom's husband now—is *not* the stepfather I was afraid of growing up."

Emotional Distance in Marriage

After we settled in, everything seemed fine until I began to notice changes in my husband's behavior and routines. Previously, he associated with a questionable individual, which led to his brief incarceration. His recent actions rekindled the same feelings I experienced back then, prompting my questions. He responded with anger and insults, and in my frustration, I retaliated, aiming to hurt him more than he was hurting me.

It seemed as though the man I married had become my adversary, but I couldn't understand how or why. I was overwhelmed, confused about how we had gone from being deeply in love to constant arguments and hostility.

Feeling lost, I discussed our marital problems with just about anyone in my family who would listen to me rant. So often I said I wanted to divorce him, passionately too, I was over it, then I wasn't, then I was. Crazy, right!

Without any evidence, just the fruitless seeds of a single and probably miserable, female neighbor, I began accusing him of cheating every time he left the house outside of work hours. The silly part is, I believed it, wholeheartedly too, and maybe that had a lot to do with the fact that I was feeling guilty about wanting to end our marriage while lacking the courage to say it to his face.

What I learned is that I was projecting the things I was feeling onto him without even realizing it, heck, I didn't know that was a thing that people do, and it is a common thing. Although he isn't a philanderer, at the same time he wasn't blameless in my feeling the way I was feeling, but he wasn't responsible for my behavior either.

Self-projecting is unconsciously attributing your own thoughts, feelings, or behaviors onto other people. Essentially seeing your own internal issues reflected in others, often as a defense mechanism to avoid confronting those aspects of yourself.

The Bible and Self-Projection

I wouldn't be me if I didn't refer to the bible about this topic. While the bible does not explicitly use the term "self-projection" or "self-projecting", it does give us many instances that helps us to see that this behavior has been a thing long before it was named in our worldly psychological definition.

    Think of the story of Cain and Abel when jealousy was at play. Abel was completely blameless in what Cain was feeling, but Cain murdered his brother. Isn't this the same way people are today?! Jealousy, strife, envy, ego, and pride. This happens in marriages too, because the closest person to us is typically the person that we see as the worst of self, and that can spark self-projection.

The word of God teaches us humility and avoiding pride. Galatians 2:20 and Philippians 1:6 teaches us that our identity is in Christ, and we can grow past feelings and emotions that come with and/or from self-projection.

Why, because when we set aside all of those thoughts that

makes us think so highly or lowly of ourselves, we are all equal.

Finding Myself Again in the World

The victimized version of me read the bible for validation of my pain and suffering. The problems that I wanted to overcome were not what I focused on, I searched for more of what made the person that caused the problems the perpetual villain in my daily life.

When I learned through reading the bible with a childlike enthusiasm for the truth, things changed. I was able to receive the Word as plain truth.

I was able to release the hurt, the victimhood, and the inner turmoil that had been with me for so many years of my life.

"Learning to love myself wasn't about bubble baths or Instagram quotes — it was about facing what the traumas, owning what was mine, and trusting Yeshua with the rest."

Trauma Meets Love

The union between my husband and I was quite an adventure, both exciting and massively frustrating, dare I say that it is "... quite possibly one of the most beautifully aggravating and transformative experiences of my life..." We are complete opposites, but when we hooked up, we felt we were a great match based on youthful beliefs and values, or maybe it was the things we believed while still aching from our traumas.

For me, this has been more difficult than I had allowed anyone close to me know in the past. I struggled with feeling unaccepted as a so-called black person, even amongst family, because I married someone of a different complexion and background. I have been told on many occasions that my "black card" has been revoked, which is one of those things that is very mediocre to me because my skin is not something that mattered as much to me as my soul, my spirit, my total fruitfulness as a young woman trying to learn to live in the best way I could find.

I did know that it is absolutely ridiculous that we have to deal with this nonsense, and with certain outspoken public figures whose commentary adds fuel to division rather than healing, who also happen to be unmarried. They make it worse with their personal opinions plastered over the internet.

We already have many issues involving our identities in darker skin due to the falsehoods that is so-called 'black' and so-called 'white', and while people continue to be racist. The ones of us who know better, battle when and where it is appropriate to speak about the fake races.

When my husband and I first met, I wasn't physically attracted to him, and his skin color wasn't a factor. My preferences leaned toward men with an aggressive appearance—those who worked out, had a naturally fit physique, and exuded a certain swagger. Oh boy, was I silly!

He was nineteen, while I was twenty-three. He was tall, skinny, with a long ponytail, and wore a flannel shirt that, for some reason, I found unattractive. This was a stark contrast to my usual type. I was also quite skinny, which I jokingly thought was reminiscent of starting a fire with sticks. Lol!

And when he and I had our first conversation, I told him that I had two younger sisters. He said, "I don't want your damn sister, I want you." I liked that. But, more than his very frank words, I felt safe in his presence, and I had no idea why. I mean, he didn't appear to be threatening at all, nor did he have the demeanor of someone who would be whatever I thought was my type.

"At the time, I was technically in a relationship—or maybe even engaged. Either way, that situation was already fading, and looking back, he's not worth more ink.

About two weeks after meeting that young man, I couldn't shake the feeling of safety, and my curiosity grew stronger. I needed to learn more about him. So, after a quick call to my sister-in-law, Stephanie, I found myself back around him, quickly getting to know him better.

He is a hugger, I was not, he is a kisser, I was not. He was very passionate, and I was not. We just did not match, yet he would not let me go, and I didn't want him to. I was like a baby bird with a broken wing, and he was compassionate enough to care for me.

Even with his anger problem, I didn't judge him since I carried a similar burden. And the conversations we had that absolutely won me over, we matched in trauma, we matched in values, and we matched in desires. Ultimately, we nurtured one another's hurts and pains, and we fantasized about being the peace for each other that we both needed.

As the months rolled by, on my days off of work at U.S. Support Company, and his days off from school at Vo-Tech, now Northwest Louisiana Technical Community College, we would often walk through Cherokee Park, either going to the corner store, or just walking and talking, often holding hands, and at times, being silly.

On one of those walks, three Shreveport police cruisers swerved up on us, which was surprising since I was sure we didn't commit any crimes. They told us that someone called and said that a white man was harassing a black girl.

Of course, we told them that we were together and just walking to the store. They separated us, he was questioned about his tattoos and was asked with an undertone of accusation if he was in a gang. They claimed his tats looked like gang tattoos, but his tats are his name in Old Roman.

They asked me if I knew him, I said, yes. They asked me his address, I told them. They asked me his first and last name, I told them. The white male and female officers were satisfied with our answers, but the one black male officer wanted to keep questioning me while looking at my boo with disgust, which is when I began to get irritated.

He repeated a couple of the previous questions to which I replied with the same answers in a sassy and aggravated tone, then finally the white lady cop said something to him, then he left us alone.

Needless to say, we were both very irritated with that exchange. I was in complete shock honestly. I had no idea that a black man, cop or not, would behave that way. I'd get it if I was his daughter and he was my racist dad, but having no relation besides complexion made his behavior weird to me.

"That moment reminded me that love doesn't shield you from judgment—but it can strengthen you to stand through it."

Throughout the years, I noticed mild racism from strangers, mostly black men, but sometimes older white women. Honey, you'd think I stole their man. Lol!

Another time, in 2010, after I had given birth to our second child, Myah. Barely sleeping and poor diet is no way to bring a child into the world, but she made it, My granny and my uncle Ron prayed over us in the hospital hours before she was born, and I am confident that those prayers were the plea that helped to save my baby girl. She was tiny though.

Just before she was born, my nurse injected me with steroids because after three shots in my back side failed to stop the contractions, it was necessary for the medical team to deliver her early.

Immediately after she was born and in the little incubator her doctor suggested a concoction that he called "Hulk Juice" which was a mixture of steroids and other additives that he said was necessary for her to survive. The doctor said she will be big, but she will be healthy, so we agreed, and we were told that she needed to stay in NICU for nine weeks, she was actually out in four weeks.

Another time, we were walking to the hospital because we had transportation problems, none, we didn't have a vehicle. As we walked down Kings Highway towards Louisiana State University Health Science Center, now called Oshner LSU, an older black man was passing us. He looked at me and said, "you ought to be ashamed of yourself with that white man." As if he was a better choice, ha!

Never in my life have I been offended by who some stranger

chooses to do life with, it is not my business, nor do I care.

Here's what I love about being united with a person that comes from a different walk of life. It has broadened my horizons to learn life from other perspectives, seeing and experiencing things with a childlike outlook.

I've learned that it is pretty delightful to allow myself to embrace my husband's family and their way of life.

There were many associations with people throughout the years, but there has not been true friendships up to this point in my life. I've often wondered why people don't like me, but I had to face the fact that other people may not be the issue.

It is very possible that I have made people uncomfortable, or I offended them. Here's why; I recently found out that I hurt a close family friend years ago.

I was very paranoid about someone abusing my kids, I insulted him by insinuating that I didn't trust him around my babies, and I didn't, but the thing is, I didn't trust anyone outside of a hand full of my immediate family members. To be clear, I never trusted all of them either.

But it was completely uncalled for me to say that to him because he didn't know what to make of that. When he told me about this, I really felt bad, especially since I am healed now.

I apologized multiple times because I do love him like a blood brother.

"Healing helped me see how fear can make us unintentionally wound people we love—and healing also makes space for making it right."

Becoming

Years ago, I read a passage in the Bible:

"Every wise woman builds her house, but the foolish pulls it down with her hands."
— Proverbs 14:1

At first glance, it seemed straightforward. But over time, I realized that this verse held profound wisdom—a seed planted in my youth that slowly grew into a life lesson on discernment and intention.

This scripture teaches us how important it is for a woman to be intentional and cautious in building her home and relationships. A wise woman builds, protects, nurtures. A foolish woman, on the other hand, destroys with her choices, words, and actions.

That verse forced me to take a long, hard look at myself—not just as a wife, but as a woman. I had to ask myself:

Do I display foolishness?

Am I destroying my own life and relationships?

And truthfully... yes. I was.

I had to admit that I was careless with my words— aggressive with profanity, name-calling, and always needing to control the narrative. Acknowledging this was the first step toward transformation. I began to understand that I had the power to shift the atmosphere in my home by embracing wisdom, patience, and understanding. It's not an easy path—but it is a necessary one.

From there, I committed to becoming a lifelong student.

I decided to talk less and listen more. I reflected deeply on my actions and how they impacted those closest to me, especially my children and husband. I started asking questions of people I admired, listening to their stories, and learning from their experiences. I turned to books, conversations, and trusted elders for guidance.

But all roads eventually led me right back to my Bible.

Bit by bit, I began to change. It started with the 'Fruits of the

Spirit,' the first tools I added to my "Becoming" toolbox:

"Walk in the Spirit, and you shall not fulfill the lust of the flesh... But the fruit of the Spirit is love, joy, peace, long-suffering, kindness, goodness, faithfulness, gentleness, self-control. Against such there is no law."
— Galatians 5:16, 22–23

I made it my mission to practice patience and empathy,

rather than feeding my hunger to "be right." I focused on understanding others instead of defending myself.

Surprisingly, gardening also became part of my healing and growth.
It might seem off-topic, but the Bible uses planting and cultivating as metaphors constantly. One of the first scriptures that stood out to me was:

"Do not be deceived: God is not mocked, for whatever a man sows, that he will also reap."
— Galatians 6:7

This verse taught me that our words, behaviors, and choices are seeds. What we plant, we eventually harvest. And I wanted to start planting better things—on purpose.

Over time, I began to see the results of those changes. My

relationships started to strengthen. My home became more peaceful. Respect and love became the new foundation. No, I'm not perfect. But I'm not who I used to be either. I'm no longer tearing down my house. I'm building.

This journey taught me that wisdom is not a destination, it's a daily choice. A process. A rhythm. Becoming the best version of ourselves isn't just for our benefit but for the sake of everyone we love.

What I've come to realize is that "becoming wife" was never something outside of me. She was already inside me—just buried beneath trauma, intrusive thoughts, diagnoses, and pain from a broken past.

"Becoming Wife" has been a rocky, humbling road of constant decisions. With each challenge I face, I choose calm. That's how I remind myself to pray. And when I pray, I invite the Holy Spirit into the moment—so I don't act out of it.

The truth is this: the same way we learned destructive behaviors, we can unlearn them. We can replace them with truth, with fruit, and with actions that lead to a life of peace, joy, and legacy.

My Lane

In my mid to late teenage years and into my early twenties, my main objective was simple: work for pay and go clubbing. The real goal? To drink myself into a blackout just so I wouldn't have to think about my life. If I made it to bed, great. If not, that was fine too.

The ugly truth is that I believed my life existed solely to be abused and used—just someone else's sexual gratification. That lie was planted deep inside me, and it shaped how I saw myself and how I allowed others to treat me.

When I was six, we moved to California. I came back to Shreveport at nineteen because I missed my mom and siblings deeply. I was completely alone in the mean streets of L.A. and convinced I wouldn't live past twenty-five. For years after my 25th birthday, each birthday felt like a miracle.

I had two completely different club personalities. One night at the old teen club *The Mansion*—which honestly might have been a brothel in its earlier days—I was wild. Like, *dancing-on-the-speakers* wild. I looked like I was on something (I wasn't), acting more like an untamed animal than a girl trying to have a good time. Other nights, I was quiet, distant, and withdrawn.

Looking back, I believe the environment, the people's energy, and the music pulled me into a dark place at times.

    Despite the chaos, some of my favorite memories are from being with my family and close family friends. That part of my past brings joy and laughter. I'm related to some characters, and we definitely know how to get to the jokes! Not everything needs fixing. I've learned to love people as they are—while also setting healthy boundaries.

For example, if you've got a relative with sticky fingers, you don't leave them near your purse or leave them alone in your house. Their feelings might get hurt, but so do yours when something goes missing. Boundaries aren't disrespectful; they're responsible.

My biggest inner battle was holding onto "Old Valerie," Cali, Lil'

Bit, the version of me people liked more. The turn-up queen. She popped tops, dropped it low, and hung out 'til the sun came up. She was bitter, angry, broken, and didn't even know it. That girl thought she was living the best life. What I didn't know then is that the seeds of wisdom planted in my youth had good roots, and they were being watered, little by little.

In my first book *Mended Crown: A Girl Exalted*, in Chapter 7 titled *Consciousness*, I shared an experience of what I now understand as a SEIZURE/RAGE episode. At the time, I didn't know how to explain it. But I knew I was under demonic attack. Still, I asked the age-old question: *Why me?*

From 2015 to July 2022, I was praying, reading the Bible here and there, especially when I had problems. I was trying to be a godly woman, but I didn't feel like I was getting anywhere.

And then, *Yeshua showed up*.

On July 3, 2022, feeling anxious and depressed, I was scrolling through Facebook and stumbled across a video of a woman talking about writing books. Her energy caught my attention. I heard, deep within, "click the link." I did. Her name was Titanya Johnson, better known as Lady Ty the Great, founder of *Greater U University*, an online writing course.

But God had more in store. Lady Ty introduced me to something beyond writing: the *Master Life Discipleship* group. That was the flame that lit a fire in me for truly seeking the Word of God.

THE MASTER LIFE COURSE, CREATED BY LIFEWAY, INCLUDES FOUR POWERFUL WORKBOOKS:

1. THE DISCIPLE'S CROSS

2. THE DISCIPLE'S PERSONALITY

3. **The Disciple's Victory**

4. **The Disciple's Mission**

Each is a six-week journey into deepening your relationship with Christ, learning to pray purposefully, and hearing the Holy Spirit clearly.

At first, I procrastinated. I dipped my toe in. But about five weeks in, I finally committed. I started taking it *one day at a time*. And as I wrote, *Mended Crown*, an incredibly emotional journey. Those discipleship lessons kept me grounded in with daily prayer and meditation. Every tear, every memory, every time I thought I couldn't keep writing, I was able to pray and keep going. I firmly believe I couldn't have finished that book, or the course, with my own strength.

Facing problems head-on wasn't something I learned growing up. In toxic environments, you learn to *survive*, not problem-solve. But as a wife and mother, that mindset had to go. I had to become present, responsible, and healed.

My healing truly began in 2015 when I decided the only person who could change my life was *me*. First step? Stop going to clubs. Now, don't get me wrong, I love hanging out with my family. But clubbing wasn't it anymore.

These days, I look forward to family barbecues, fish fries, Memorial Day gatherings, and whatever else we come up with. Reunions don't happen often, but I'm hoping for more.

Identity Beyond Titles

Over the years of being someone's wife, I've learned something powerful: being a wife is not my entire identity.

I am *so much more* than a wife. More than a mother. More than a daughter, sister, or aunt.

I am **encouragement**.
I am a **nurturer**.
I love **unconditionally**.
I hope to **heal**.
I seek **truth**.
And **our Savior is the absolute**

best guide of who I am learning to 'Become' as *Valerie*.

Conclusion

When you listen to some of our elders' complaints and their delights about their own unions, we can find the gems they drop for us. Some of our elders may give some wonderful wisdom about relationships, friendships, and marriage. Others may tell us the most awful vile things, I've heard some of both types of stories.

There are some distorted outlooks, traumas, and the differences of values, standards, knowledge, wisdom, accurate information, and misogyny that leads to many of the challenges. The fact is that some folks are salty at relationships, friendships, and marriage, while others love and respect their families, friends, and spouses' similarities and differences.

In world views, marriage often involves two individuals deciding to unite based on their own interpretations and societal expectations. They tend to rely on their feelings, emotions, and personal desires as their primary guides. Balancing self-exploration, family, and friendship can add to problems.

On the other hand, godly marriages depend on the wisdom and direction of the Holy Spirit. By seeking the Holy Spirit throughout the marriage, couples can maintain their covenant with Yahweh.

Many people enter marriage for reasons that fall outside of biblical principles, such as prioritizing romantic love, making a public commitment, succumbing to external pressures, wanting a stable family life, adhering to societal norms, or seeking titles and comforts they believe will be beneficial.

Biblical reasons for marriage include companionship, procreation, redemption, reflecting Yahweh's love, modeling Yahweh's covenant, serving as a testimony to the gospel, establishing a family foundation, and providing a space for intimacy.

The Bible defines marriage as a covenant rather than a contract. A covenant is built on trust and unlimited responsibility and is unbreakable, while a contract is based on distrust, limited liability, and can be nullified by mutual agreement.

I realized that becoming wife was never about me cooking better, looking better, doing better, and putting up a front for others to see. Becoming wife was being my best self, realizing who I am as a believer, and not as what the world sees me as. Becoming his being happy with the eyes looking back at you in the mirror. It is taking the time to learn oneself, because we've reflected on all the things over the courses of our lives that have taken place, to shape and build us, good and bad. Becoming is learning, understanding, and growing individually.

Wife to me means being or becoming whole, it means reflecting on the things that have broken or destroyed you, or have built you, so that you can exist in a marriage as 100% of who you are, to bring 100% of your skills to the marriage.

There are times when one of you will be at a lower percentage, and vice versa, that is why being healed and whole matters.

In my own union, my husband has a way with me that I cannot explain, there is something about the way he is with me that I have never understood. Maybe it is the same safety I have felt ever since the day I met him.

The safety I felt then still remains the same nearly twenty years later. But it had been clouded by all of the offensive language and multiple traumas I was dealing with. Being a victim of childhood sexual abuse, physical abuse, and emotional abuse paired with teenage pregnancies and not knowing where my children were, played the majority role in my presence in our marriage.

I didn't realize that I had no idea what being someone's wife was, my idea of wife life was far from reality. The image in my mind was quite romanticized and immature due to my youthful enthusiasm that lacked training and proper preparation.

And here's the thing, I married a man that is truly old fashioned at his core. He wasn't raised like my brothers, cooking, cleaning, doing his own laundry, no, none of that, those are things that were done by his mother and grandmother. Oh boy, it made me furious at times.

I could not understand why a grown man wasn't handling basic skills such as laundry.

Here's what I found out over time. I don't cut grass, nor do I trim hedges or grab the chainsaw to cut and maintain trees on the property, I have never had to change the oil in my car or replace a tire, and I have never paid for that stuff either. We live in an area that does not have trash pick-up, my husband and son are the ones who manage and burn all of our waste.

We each had things we were good at, shaped by our upbringings and the skills we developed. It was a revelation to see that what seemed unfair was actually just different.

Marriage, I learned, is about finding balance and appreciating the strengths each person brings to the relationship.

As I grew to understand this, I began to see the beauty in our partnership. My husband's traditional ways taught me patience and respect for his values, while I showed him the importance of sharing and adapting. We both grew from our differences, learning to support and uplift each other in ways we hadn't expected.

And so, I learned to cherish the small acts of love and compromise that define a strong marriage. Every day became an opportunity to communicate better, to laugh together, and to build a life that combines our unique backgrounds and dreams. It wasn't always easy, but the journey taught me that true partnership is about embracing both the challenges and the joys and growing together with understanding and love.

So, I repeat, Becoming Wife is growing from girl to woman, we learn, we embody, we change, we blossom into the flower that is Wife. We do this by keeping the knowledge we learn and finding the biblical balance, and that gives us some Godly wisdom. And I will add my personal opinion to it. As a wife, turning up and twerking is not becoming of a wife, no respectable man wants to see his wife behaving in that way, unless of course, it is behind closed doors with him only. Furthermore, we are to respect and value ourselves.

Becoming Wife was not me simply being better for my husband. We, married people, set an example for individuals who are ready, curious, or in the future, will think about getting married. Becoming a wife is remembering that my union is a lifelong commitment between he and I, and Yahweh, it is both religious and civil, it requires for both of us to continue to consent to our union, and to sex too, (please never weaponize sex with your spouse) and finally, it was me remembering my vows. As a wife, I understands that I am a part of the body of Christ and in that is responsibility, it is covenant with the Most High.

About the Author

Valerie J. Pacheco is a wife, mother, and faith-filled storyteller from Shreveport, Louisiana. With honesty and heart, she writes to help women grow into their God-given identity—one choice, one lesson, and one season at a time. *Becoming Wife* is her personal journey of hindsight, healing, and becoming the "good thing" she was created to be.

Written, edited, & manufactured by Valerie J. Pacheco

Email me: goodstuff.natural@gmail.com

For more writings visit:
www.goodstuffbyvaleriepacheco.org

www.ingramcontent.com/pod-product-compliance
Lightning Source LLC
Chambersburg PA
CBHW071700170426
43195CB00039B/2409